First World War
and Army of Occupation
War Diary
France, Belgium and Germany

29 DIVISION
87 Infantry Brigade
Devonshire Regiment
51st (Y.S.) Battalion
12 March 1919 - 31 October 1919

WO95/2305/4

The Naval & Military Press Ltd
www.nmarchive.com
Published in association with The National Archives

Published by

The Naval & Military Press Ltd

Unit 10 Ridgewood Industrial Park,

Uckfield, East Sussex,

TN22 5QE England

Tel: +44 (0) 1825 749494

www.naval-military-press.com

www.nmarchive.com

This diary has been reprinted in facsimile from the original. Any imperfections are inevitably reproduced and the quality may fall short of modern type and cartographic standards.

© **Crown Copyright**
Images reproduced by permission of The National Archives, London, England, 2015.

Contents

Document type	Place/Title	Date From	Date To
Heading	WO95/2305/4 51 Battalion Devonshire Regiment Mar 19-Oct 19		
Heading	Southern (Late 29th) Divn. 87th Infy Bde 51st Bn Divn Regt Mar-Oct 1919		
War Diary	Moullwind	12/03/1919	15/03/1919
War Diary	Burscheid	15/03/1919	24/04/1919
War Diary	Burg.	27/04/1919	26/05/1919
War Diary	Hilgen	27/05/1919	19/06/1919
War Diary	Lolingen	20/06/1919	30/06/1919
War Diary	Hilgen	01/07/1919	31/07/1919
Miscellaneous	Special Order. 51st Battalion The Devonshire Regiment.	24/07/1919	24/07/1919
War Diary	Hilgen	01/08/1919	15/08/1919
War Diary	Dellbruck	16/08/1919	29/08/1919
War Diary	Hilgen	30/08/1919	27/09/1919
War Diary	Burg.	28/09/1919	21/10/1919
War Diary	Burscheid.	22/10/1919	29/10/1919
War Diary	Ermelskirchen	30/10/1919	31/10/1919

WO 95/2305/4

51 Battalion Devonshire Regiment

Nov '14 – Oct '19

SOUTHERN (LATE 29TH) DIVN.
87TH INFY BDE

51ST BN DEVON REGT
MAR - OCT 1919

SOUTHERN DIV.

Army Form C. 2118.

WAR DIARY
or
INTELLIGENCE SUMMARY.
(Erase heading not required.)

Instructions regarding War Diaries and Intelligence Summaries are contained in F.S. Regs. Part II. and the Staff Manual respectively. Title pages will be prepared in manuscript.

Place	Date	Hour	Summary of Events and Information	Remarks and references to Appendices
Mulheim	12.3.19		Train arrived at Mulheim at 0435. Breakfasts were taken at the Station and detraining commenced at 0535. The Battalion then proceeded to billets in the town taking over two schools. The men bathed at the Public Baths in the afternoon. The Commanding Officer motored to Burscheid, Headquarters of 57th Infantry Brigade.	Star Bearer Mar – Oct 1919
	13.3.19		The day was spent in cleaning up Band rooms	
	14.3.19	0900	One Platoon of 'A' Company went to Burscheid. Party, by Motor Lorry. Major C.L. Swinson D.S.O. 2nd I/C was in charge. The Quartermaster Lt. A.T. Smith Lt. C.E. Reed and one Other Rank Company accompanied the Party to arrange billets, etc.	
	15.3.19	0900	The Battalion marched to Burscheid and took over from the 3rd Bn B.S.L.I. Running Party of the 57th Inf. Bde. Two men who were left put on the march were left behind as Unable in order. Lunch was served at 1245 from Travelling Kitchens.	
Burscheid	15.3.19/ 15.15		Battalion arrived at Burscheid and Proceeded to billets. Battalion attended Church Parade.	
	16.3.19			

Army Form C. 2118.

WAR DIARY
or
INTELLIGENCE SUMMARY.
(Erase heading not required.)

Instructions regarding War Diaries and Intelligence Summaries are contained in F. S. Regs., Part II. and the Staff Manual respectively. Title pages will be prepared in manuscript.

Place	Date	Hour	Summary of Events and Information	Remarks and references to Appendices
Busschud	17.3.19		Lieut. A.E. Prudy was detached to Headquarters 87th Inf. Bde. to understudy the Staff Captain.	
	18.3.19		15 Other Ranks were attached to the Battalion from the Band of 2nd S.W.B. Lieut. Parsons took over duties of Brigade Education Officer temporary.	
	19.3.19		Day spent in clearing up and re-organising billets etc.	
	20.3.19		Brigadier General Commanding 87th Brigade visited the Battalion and inspected the Transport. Brigadier General Lucas took over command of 87th Brigade vice Brigadier General Jackson. Refixed H.A. Lets & 8 other ranks proceeded to Cologne to act as Train Guard.	
	21.3.19	1000	Major General Henneker C.O.C. Southern Division inspected the Battalion clear-up in mass, with Transport etc. on The R.E. Football ground.	
	22.3.19		Re-organising and General Parade.	
	23.3.19		Church Parade at 1100	
	24.3.19		Parades under Company arrangements	
	25.3.19		& Re-organisation — 10 Other Ranks proceeded on Guard Duties at Divisional Headquarters	
	26.3.19			
	27.3.19		1 Other Rank & Col. Wright proceded to Cologne to take part in trials for Army of	

Army Form C. 2118.

WAR DIARY
or
INTELLIGENCE SUMMARY.
(Erase heading not required.)

Instructions regarding War Diaries and Intelligence Summaries are contained in F. S. Regs., Part II. and the Staff Manual respectively. Title pages will be prepared in manuscript.

Place	Date	Hour	Summary of Events and Information	Remarks and references to Appendices
Burschied	27.3.19		Occupation troops Burnley Team.	
			"D" Coy moved into Billets at Stickenberg about 2 miles N.W. of Burscheid.	
	28.3.19		Parades under Company arrangements & re-organization of Battalion vide O.B.	
	29.3.19		1919. Conference between Officer Commanding and Company Commanders in regard to Individual Training, to commence on 1st prox.	
	30.3.19	1100	Church Parade	
	31.3.19		Parades under Company arrangements and re-organisation	

WAR DIARY
or
INTELLIGENCE SUMMARY.
(Erase heading not required.)

Army Form C. 2118.

Place	Date	Hour	Summary of Events and Information	Remarks and references to Appendices
Burscheid.	1.4.19.		Routine, Training and Games.	
Burscheid.	2.4.19	9-11.	Battalion Route March with Band and Drums. BURSCHEID to LUCKENBERG, thence through BLASBERG, HERKENSIEFEN, to BURSCHEID. On returning to BURSCHEID the Battalion marched past the Divisional Commander, who arrived in BURSCHEID during the absence of the Battalion. The Divisional Commander subsequently inspected Bathing arrangements.	
Burscheid.	3.4.19. 4.4.19. 5.4.19.		Routine, Training and Games.	
"	6.4.19.	1100.	Church Parade in the Lutheran Church. In the afternoon a "Rugger" Match was played against the 52nd. Battalion Devonshire Regiment at BURG. The party from this Battalion proceeded by motor lorry.	
"	7.4.19.		Routine, Training and Games.	
"	8.4.19.	" 1400.	Inspection of the Battalion by the Corps Commander Lieut.General Sir Claud Jacobs, K.C.B. K.C.M.G. In the afternoon an Orchestral Concert was given by the R.E. Orchestra.	
B	9.4.19		Routine, Training and Games.	
"	10.4.19		Lieut.Colonel D, E, D. Sword, D.S.O., left for No.56 C.C.S. for medical attention.	
"	11.4.19.		Routine, Training and Games.	

Army Form C. 2118.

WAR DIARY
or
INTELLIGENCE SUMMARY.
(Erase heading not required.)

Instructions regarding War Diaries and Intelligence Summaries are contained in F. S. Regs., Part II. and the Staff Manual respectively. Title pages will be prepared in manuscript.

Place	Date	Hour	Summary of Events and Information	Remarks and references to Appendices
Burscheid.	12.4.19	1000.	The Battalion was inspected by Brigadier General C. H. Tindale Lucas, C.M.G. D.S.O. The morning was wet. The Brigadier General expressed satisfaction at the improvement shown.	
"		1100.	A Lecture was given by Mr. T, E. Wing, the subject being "How the Navy helped the Army to win the War" A number of all ranks from this Battalion occupied seats allotted.	
"	13.4.19.-1930	1030.	Conference of Commanding Officers with Adjutants at Brigade Headquarters. Principally relative to the distribution of Personnel and Effects of the 53rd. Battalion, The Devonshire Regiment. Instructions received for all Officers to wear arms, and for general precautions for the protection of Officer Personnel.	
"	14.4.19.		The Billets of "B" and "C" Companies were inspected by Brigadier General C, H. Tindale Lucas, C.M.G. D.S.O.	
"	15.4.19.		Routine, Training and Games.	
"	16.4.19.	1200.	A draft of 7 Officers and 253 Other Ranks of 53rd. Battalion Devonshire Regiment arrived, and were accommodated in pre-arranged billets.	
"	17.4.19.		Lieut-Colonel H. T. Dobbin, D.S.O reported for duty and assumed Command of the Battalion.	
"	18.4.19.	1130.	Church Parade in the Lutheran Church. The Church of England Party paraded with a strength of 23 Officers and 510 Other Ranks, Major C. T. Simcox D.S.O. acted as President of a Board for examination of Rifle Ranges in Brigade Area.	

Army Form C. 2118.

WAR DIARY
or
INTELLIGENCE SUMMARY.
(Erase heading not required.)

Instructions regarding War Diaries and Intelligence Summaries are contained in F. S. Regs., Part II. and the Staff Manual respectively. Title pages will be prepared in manuscript.

Place	Date	Hour	Summary of Events and Information	Remarks and references to Appendices
Burscheid.	18.4.19 (contd)		A Shooting Match in the afternoon between teams of (a) Officers, (b) W.Os. and N.C.Os. The latter won by 1 point.	
"	19.4.19.		A shot was fired, apparently at the Battalion Quarter Guard, at about 2145. Brigade Headquarters and the D.A.P.M. were advised and immediate enquiries were instituted, but without any result.	
"	20.4.19.	1130.	Church Parade 4th Lutheran Church.	
"	21.4.19.		Observed as a Holiday. An Association Football Match in the afternoon between the 51st. Battalion Devonshire Regiment and The Royal Engineers. Result 1 - 0. The Commanding Officer proceeded to BURG to discuss details of the forthcoming Move with the Commanding Officer of the 52nd Battalion Devonshire Regiment.	
"	22.4.19.		Orders received for this Battalion to take over duties on the 2nd Southern Infantry Brigade Perimeter on the 26th instant.	
"	23.4.19.		Major D. C. D. Sword D.S.O. rejoined the Battalion from No. 36 C.C.S. LINDENTHAL. Commanders of Companies to do duty on Perimeter left for residence in the Line with the Companies of the 1/5th Battalion and 52nd. Battalion Devonshire Regiment, presently doing duty.	
"	24.4.19.		Quartermaster, Signalling Officer, Transport Officer and others, proceeded to BURG preparatory to taking over. Detailed Battalion Movement Orders published.	

Army Form C. 2118.

WAR DIARY
or
INTELLIGENCE SUMMARY.
(Erase heading not required.)

Instructions regarding War Diaries and Intelligence Summaries are contained in F. S. Regs., Part II. and the Staff Manual respectively. Title pages will be prepared in manuscript.

Place	Date	Hour	Summary of Events and Information	Remarks and references to Appendices
Burgsheid.	25.4.19.		Advance Party despatched to BURG. Concert in the evening by Miss Bensusan's Party. This attracted a packed "House" and was greatly enjoyed.	
Burgsheid.	26.4.19.	0830.	"B" and "C" Companies marched out from BURSCHEID, timed to arrive at PREYERS MUHLE and VIERINGHAUSEN, respectively, at 0630 to relieve the Companies of 1/5th and 52nd Battalions, after Dinners. Headquarters and "A" and "D" Companies, with the balance of Transport, marched out from BURSCHEID at 0930. Variable weather was encountered on the march – with some rain and hail, but generally the weather was favourable to marching and there were no cases of falling out reported. Mobility was good with the exception of one Travelling Kitchen, which was, however, patched-up to finish the journey. BURG was reached at 1245 and "A" Company marched on to UNTERBURG whilst Battalion Headquarters and "D" Company were billetted in SCHLOSS.	
Burg.	27-4-19.		There was a fall of snow overnight. The Battalion spent the day in a general clearing up of billets and precincts. The Commanding Officer and 2nd i/c visited the Companies on Perimeter.	
Burg.	28-4-19.	1000.	The General Officer Commanding 2nd Southern Infantry Brigade arrived, accompanied by an R.E. Officer, and after picking up the Commanding Officer and an Interpreter, the party proceeded to the VIERINGHAUSEN SALIENT, being joined at the HATCHERIES by Officer Commanding "C" Company. The Line was inspected and definite positions for wiring chosen.	
Burg.	29-4-19.	1430. 1700.	Commander Everard. R.N. lectured on "Submarine Warfare", and delivered an amusing and interesting lecture. The Battalion Sports Committee met at BURG.	
Burg.	30-4-19.		General Routine and Training. Individual Musketry Training and revision commenced; also Pool Shooting.	

Army Form C. 2118.

WAR DIARY
or
INTELLIGENCE SUMMARY.
(Erase heading not required.)

Instructions regarding War Diaries and Intelligence Summaries are contained in F. S. Regs., Part II. and the Staff Manual respectively. Title pages will be prepared in manuscript.

Place	Date	Hour	Summary of Events and Information	Remarks and references to Appendices
Burg.	1.5.19.		Routine& Training.	
	2.5.19.		-do-	
	3.5.19.		-do-	
	4.5.19.		Church Parade at DORTMUNDER HOFF Hall, UNTERBURG. Battalion Headquarter Company and "D" and "A" Companies attended.	
	5.5.19.		Orders received for withdrawal of Perimeter line to a line approximately KELLERS HAMMER westward to KAISER WILHELM Bridge.	
		1145.	Visit of Divisional Commander who arrived at 1145 and departed at 1245. Wiring of new Perimeter line commenced by "C" Company assisted by "B" Company.	
		2215.	A German civilian was shot in the arm at 2215 last night at VIERINGHAUSEN whilst attempting to evade British Sentries.	
	6.5.19.		Defensive and Advanced Guard Schemes for the Sector of the 2nd Southern Infantry Brigade received and Operation Orders Nos. 1 and 2, together with Administration Orders, issued.	
	7.5.19.	1545.	Visit to the SCHLOSS by Field Martial H.R.H. Arthur, Duke of Connaught, K.G., K.T., etc. Arrived at 1545 and departed at 1615. Guard of Honour mounted by this Battalion the Commander being complimented by His Royal Highness.	
	8.5.19.		A shot was fired at the British Sentry at KELLERS HAMMER last night the shot passing through the Sentry Box. The removal of Government Stores from the VIERINGHAUSEN line commenced. Wire received from Divisional Commander congratulating the Guard of Honour provided to the Duke of Connaught yesterday. Summer weather.	

Army Form C. 2118.

WAR DIARY
or
INTELLIGENCE SUMMARY.
(Erase heading not required.)

Instructions regarding War Diaries and Intelligence Summaries are contained in F.S. Regs., Part II. and the Staff Manual respectively. Title pages will be prepared in manuscript.

Place	Date	Hour	Summary of Events and Information	Remarks and references to Appendices
BURG	9.5.19.		Withdrawal of Line and all Government property and relief of "C" by "D" Company completed by 1130. Lieut. C. L. G. Mackay-Forbes to be Acting Captain as from 15.2.19.	
	10.5.19.		"A" Company relieved "B" Company on the Right Sector of the Perimeter line the relief being completed by 1100. Brigade Staff ride on Defensive Scheme.	
	11.5.19.	1000.	Church Parade at UNTERBURG.	
	12.5.19.		Routine, Training and Games.	
	13.5.19.		-do-	
	14.5.19.	0900.	Spotting practice by R.A.F. "T" signals exposed on Perimeter line.	
		1100.	Lecture by The Venerable Archdeacon Jones at UNTERBURG; subject "British Character Builders". Wrestling match between Lieut. W. E. Hayes and S/S/M. Thorpe, R.A.M.C., claiming Championship of the British Army of the Rhine, resulting in an easy win for Lieut. Hayes.	
	15.5.19.		Routine, Training and Games.	
	16.5.19.		Conference of Commanding Officers at Brigade Headquarters. First Cricket match of the season played between Headquarters and "C" Companies at UNTERBURG, in the afternoon.	
		1630.	Marshal Foch visited the SCHLOSS, arriving at 1630 and departing at 1650.	

Army Form C. 2118.

WAR DIARY
or
INTELLIGENCE SUMMARY.
(Erase heading not required.)

Instructions regarding War Diaries and Intelligence Summaries are contained in F. S. Regs., Part II. and the Staff Manual respectively. Title pages will be prepared in manuscript.

Place	Date	Hour	Summary of Events and Information	Remarks and references to Appendices
BURG.	17.5.19.		Lieut.Colonel V. L. M. Pearson D.S.O., Commanding 1/5th Batln. Devonshire Regiment visited the Perimeter line preparatory to relief on the 24th.	
	18.5.19.	1100.	Church Parade at UNTERBURG. Major D. G. D. Sword, D.S.O. who commanded the Battalion until relieved by Lieut.Colonel H. T. Dobbin D.S.O., on 17th ultimo, proceeded to England to rejoin his Regiment.	
	19.5.19.		The Regimental Band played on the Perimeter line, at PREYERS MUHLE, in the afternoon. Promotions published to fill vacancies in non-commissioned ranks.	
	20.5.19.		1 Case of Scarlet Fever reported. Billet quarantined. The Brigade Commander inspected the Right Sector of the Perimeter line. Wood fire near KEHLERS HAMMER. The Battalion assisted in extinguishing the fire.	
	21.5.19.		Wood fire on Western side of KAISER WILHELM Bridge. Troops of this Battalion assisted in extinguishing the fire.	
	22.5.19.		Relief of this Battalion postponed for one week from 24th instant. Warning received of possible move into un-occupied German territory. Preliminary Movement Order issued. Regimental Band played at Officers Sports Club, LINDENTHAL.	
	23.5.19.	0930.	Conference of Commanding Officers at Brigade Headquarters. Orders received for relief of Perimeter to be carried out on 26th instant. Guard sent to Divisional Headquarters.	
	24.5.19.		Brigade Commander inspected the Perimeter line.	

Army Form C. 2118.

WAR DIARY
or
INTELLIGENCE SUMMARY.
(Erase heading not required.)

Instructions regarding War Diaries and Intelligence Summaries are contained in F.S. Regs., Part II. and the Staff Manual respectively. Title pages will be prepared in manuscript.

Place	Date	Hour	Summary of Events and Information	Remarks and references to Appendices
BURG.	25.5.19.		Operation Order No.3 issued.	
	26.5.19.		Battalion moved to HILGEN being relieved by the 1/5th Battalion The Devonshire Regiment. Left BURG at 1000; arrived HILGEN 1200 the relief of the Perimeter being completed by 1400. Operation Order No.4 issued.	
HILGEN.	27.5.19.		Ceremonial Guard Mounting instituted.	
	28.5.19.		Ceremonial Tattoo instituted.	
	29.5.19.		Routine, Training and Recreation.	
	30.5.19.		-do- -do-	
	31.5.19.		-do- -do-	
Hilgen. 2.6.19.				

[signature]
ADJUTANT.
51st BATTN. DEVONSHIRE REGT.

Lieut.Colonel.
Commanding 51st Battalion The Devonshire Regiment.

Army Form C. 2118.

WAR DIARY
or
INTELLIGENCE SUMMARY.

(Erase heading not required.)

Instructions regarding War Diaries and Intelligence Summaries are contained in F. S. Regs., Part II. and the Staff Manual respectively. Title pages will be prepared in manuscript.

Place	Date	Hour	Summary of Events and Information	Remarks and references to Appendices
Wiesen	2.6.19		Captain L. S. Petheram M.C. on course on co-operation between Artillery & Infantry	
do	2.6.19		The King's birthday. Battalion parade. The remainder of the day observed as a holiday	
do	26.9		Recruits training. Lewis guns	
do	2.6.9		Battalion N.C.Os course assembled at Headquarters consisting of all Unpaid L/Cpls. Messing and accommodation arranged for separately.	
do	2.6.9		Divisional Races. Battalion Band attended	

ORDERLY ROOM
2 JUL 1919
5TH BATTN. DEVONSHIRE

Army Form C. 2118.

WAR DIARY
or
INTELLIGENCE SUMMARY.
(Erase heading not required.)

Instructions regarding War Diaries and Intelligence Summaries are contained in F. S. Regs., Part II. and the Staff Manual respectively. Title pages will be prepared in manuscript.

Place	Date	Hour	Summary of Events and Information	Remarks and references to Appendices
Kilgau	7.6.19		Divisional Regtl. Band attended. On the return journey the lorry conveying the Band ran into a tree causing damage to several instruments.	
-do-	8.6.19	1100	Church Parade in field adjoining R.E. Dump at Kilgau.	
-do-	9.6.19		82 Other Ranks and 3 Officers on Rhine Trip.	
-do-	10.6.19		A Court Martial held on No 0136 Pte Scott W. Lovel Welsh Borderers Regt (attd 51 Bn Devon Regt)	
-do-	11.6.19		"D" Company Sports.	
-do-	12.6.19		A Company Sports. Band attended. L.O. to 2nd Southern Infantry Brigade visited the Battalion.	

Army Form C. 2118.

WAR DIARY
or
INTELLIGENCE SUMMARY.
(Erase heading not required.)

Place	Date	Hour	Summary of Events and Information	Remarks and references to Appendices
Solingen	13.6.19	0830	The Commanding Officer Lieut Colonel A J Dobbin DSO left Solingen for England. Major L Stimson DSO assumed command of the Battn	
-do-	15.6.19	1100	Church Parade in Neuenhaus	
-do-	16.6.19		The Signalling Officer Lieut A J Radley proceeded to Hospital	
-do-	17.6.19		Brigade advice received reference date for T Day & time for X hour	
-do-	18.6.19		Battalion preparing for move to Solingen. All Stores & kit dumped at Neuenhaus School	

WAR DIARY
or
INTELLIGENCE SUMMARY.

Army Form C. 2118.

Place	Date	Hour	Summary of Events and Information	Remarks and references to Appendices
Hilgen	19.6.19	0800	Battalion moved to Solingen. Route via Wermelskirchen & Burg arriving at Billeting Area in Solingen at 1255.	
			A very hot day. 6 men falling out on line of march. Divisional & Corps Commanders inspected the Battalion on line of march before entering Solingen. Major E.J. Linton D.S.O. to Hospital. Captn T.L. Hunter commanded Battalion during the absence of Major E.J. Linton, D.S.O.	
Solingen	20.6.19		To-day 1 day postponed. Lieut Colonel J.J. Collins D.S.O. reported and assumed command of Battalion	
do	21.6.19		Brigadier General C.A. Lindsell Lucas C.M.G. D.S.O visited the Battalion	

Army Form C. 2118.

WAR DIARY
or
INTELLIGENCE SUMMARY.
(Erase heading not required.)

Place	Date	Hour	Summary of Events and Information	Remarks and references to Appendices
Solingen	27.6.19	1100	Church Parade at Schwert Strasse School. Operation Order No 5 issued.	
-do-	28.6.19		Battalion Route march. Route:- Barkerhof, Gluder, Flamersheid, Orth, Wuitenhof, Wuirburg. "B" acted as Advance Guard. "D" Coy provided Rear Guard. Time of departure 0835, arriving back in Billets at 1230. Commanding Officer attended Conference at Brigade Headquarters at 1445.	

Army Form C. 2118.

WAR DIARY
or
INTELLIGENCE SUMMARY.

(Erase heading not required.)

Instructions regarding War Diaries and Intelligence Summaries are contained in F. S. Regs., Part II. and the Staff Manual respectively. Title pages will be prepared in manuscript.

51st BATTN. DEVONSHIRE REGT.

Place	Date	Hour	Summary of Events and Information	Remarks and references to Appendices
Solingen	24.6.19		Brigadier General L.F. Tindale Lucas C.M.G. D.S.O. visited the Battalion - Companies Interior Economy.	
-do-	25.6.19		Companies on Tactical Schemes.	
-do-	26.6.19	1400	Commanding Officer inspected 'C' Coy in Fighting Order.	
-do-	27.6.19		Commanding Officer inspected 'D' Coy. Band played "Retreat" in MITTLE STRASSE.	
-do-	28.6.19		Peace Treaty signed. No disturbances in SOLINGEN. Rcd Operation Order No7 iesses in move to HILDEN	
-do-	29.6.19	1115	Church Parade in Lutheran Church in KOLNER STRASSE at 1115.	
-do-	30.6.19	1030	An attended Tank Demonstration at BRUHL	

Army Form C. 2118.

WAR DIARY
or
INTELLIGENCE SUMMARY
(Erase heading not required.)

Instructions regarding War Diaries and Intelligence Summaries are contained in F. S. Regs., Part II. and the Staff Manual respectively. Title Pages will be prepared in manuscript.

Place	Date	Hour	Summary of Events and Information	Remarks and references to Appendices
HILGEN.	1.7.19.	0911.	The Battalion marched out from Solingen via Wupperhof - Herscheid - Witzhelden, arriving at Hilgen 1220. One man fell out on the line of march.	
	3.7.19.		Company Commanders Conference with Commanding Officer relative to Company Training.	
	4.7.19.		Observed as a holiday. The Battalion held Sports in the afternoon. The whole Battalion attended and teas were provided on the Sports Ground, a special prize being given for the best meal provided	
	6.7.19.	1120.	Church Parade in Church at Neuenhaus.	
	7.7.19.		Company Training commenced.	
	10.7.19.		Bathing under Battalion arrangements inaugurated in Hilgen.	
	13.7.19.	1130.	Church Parade in Church at Neuenhaus.	
	14.7.19.		Divisional Commander visited the Battalion. Educational Examination for 2nd Class Certificates was held during the day. 75 Candidates sat.	
	15.7.19.		Educational Examination for 3rd Class Certificates held during the day. 670 Candidates sat. Advice received that the Battalion proceeds to Brussels on the 19th instant, to represent the Army of the Rhine in the Belgian Peace Celebrations.	
	16.7.19.		Battalion inspected by the Divisional Commander.	
	18.7.19.		The Battalion, comprised of personnel proceeding to the Brussels Review, i.e., 20 Officers and 600 Other Ranks, inspected by Brigade Commander.	
	19.7.19.	1000.	The Battalion left by special train ex Hilgen for Brussels, 21 Officers and 600 Other Ranks	

Army Form C. 2118.

WAR DIARY
or
INTELLIGENCE SUMMARY

(Erase heading not required.)

Instructions regarding War Diaries and Intelligence Summaries are contained in F. S. Regs., Part II. and the Staff Manual respectively. Title Pages will be prepared in manuscript.

Place	Date	Hour	Summary of Events and Information	Remarks and references to Appendices
	21.7.19.		Including the Colour Party of the 1/5th Battalion and the Band of the 52nd Battalion arrived at Brussels at 2230 and marched to the Baudouin Barracks where the Battalion was accommodated. Officers were accommodated in the Palace Hotel. The following Officers accompanied the Battalion:-	
			Lieut.Col.W.J.J.Collis D.S.O. Lieut.J.Locke. 2/Lieut. G. Eggins.	
			Commanding. Lieut.F.M.Arculus. " W. E. Hayes.	
			Captain A.O.Klapka. Lieut. J. S. Vair. " R. E. Geddes.	
			Adjutant, 2nd-in-Command. Lieut. F. R. Lillicrap. " S. F. Mathews.	
			Captain F. W. Clarke. Lieut. R. V. Evans M.C. " C. R. Trelease.	
			Quartermaster. Lieut. H. D. Hooper.	
			Captain C.S.Petheram M.C. Lieut. E. W. Payne.	
			Commanding "B" Company. Lieut. L. E. Langley.	
			Captain W. G. Mills. Lieut. A. Towner.	
			Commanding "C" Company.	
			Lieut. T. H. Howe.	
			Commanding H.Q.Coy.	
			Lieut. G. A. Donaldson.	
			Commanding "A" Company.	
			Lieut. G. A. Drew.	
			Commanding "D" Company.	
			Captain Denny.	
			Medical Officer.	
			2/Lieut's Mathews and Trelease were in charge of the Colours.	
			M.Poincare arrived in Brussels in the afternoon. The Commanding Officer, Adjutant and Lieut. F. M. Arculus dined at the British Legation.	
	22.7.19.		The Battalion paraded at the Barracks at 0730 marching to the Assembly in the Rue Royal. The Battalion paraded in line at 0815 and was inspected by Lieut.General De Ceuninck, Commanding the Belgian Troops at 0900 and by His Majesty The King at 0930.	

Army Form C. 2118.

WAR DIARY
or
INTELLIGENCE SUMMARY
(Erase heading not required.)

Instructions regarding War Diaries and Intelligence Summaries are contained in F. S. Regs., Part II. and the Staff Manual respectively. Title Pages will be prepared in manuscript.

Place	Date	Hour	Summary of Events and Information	Remarks and references to Appendices
	23.7.19.	1100.	The March commenced at 0945 and terminated at 1230. The Battalion being well received throughout the march. The men bore themselves remarkably well throughout the Review, marching at attention. The morning was wet. The Commanding Officer lunched with His Majesty The King and was decorated with The Order of the Couronne. 80519 Pte. Ward of "A" Company dined at the Palace in the evening.	
	24.7.19.		The Battalion left Brussels by Special train and arrived in Hilgen at 2200 A Special Order received from the Brigade Commander complimenting the Battalion on its performance at the Brussels Peace Review.	
	25.7.19.		Photographic Groups of the Officers and of the Massed Bands, which were in Brussels, were taken. A photographic group of Warrant Officers and N.C.Os, who accompanied the Battalion to Brussels, was taken.	
	27.7.19.	1000.	Church Parade in Church at Neuenhaus.	
	28.7.19.		Company Training re-commenced. Battalion Cricket Match in the afternoon at Hilgen.	
	29.7.19.		Battalion Cricket Match in the afternoon at Hilgen.	
	30.7.19.		Battalion Cricket Team to Bonn to play match.	
	31.7.19.		Battalion Cricket Match in the afternoon at Hilgen.	

SPECIAL ORDER.

51st Battalion The Devonshire Regiment.

HILGEN.   24.7.1919.

The undermentioned letter has been received from the Brigade Commander and the Commanding Officer feels that after what has been said by higher authority there is very little to add.
He wishes, however, to thank all ranks for their loyal support and is proud to command a Battalion that has earned such high praise.

"The greatest credit is due to all ranks of 51st Devons, the Colour Party of the 5th Devons and the Band of the 52nd Devons for the highly creditable way in which they represented the British Army of the Rhine at the BRUSSELS Peace Celebrations.
The marching, cleanliness of dress and equipment, the way the men carried themselves and the general appearance of the Devon troops was most favourably critized by all those present, and surpassed that of any other Allied detachment taking part in the Celebrations.
All ranks are to be congratulated that the great amount of trouble taken by them to do credit to the British Army and the County of DEVON resulted in such well earned success."

23.7.19.
          (Sgd) K. TINDALL LUCAS.
          BRIGADIER-GENERAL.
    COMMANDING, 2nd SOUTHERN INFANTRY BRIGADE.

Hilgen.
25.7.19.   Captain.
      Adjutant, 51st Battalion The Devonshire Regiment.

51 Devons

Army Form C. 2118.

WAR DIARY
or
INTELLIGENCE SUMMARY.
(Erase heading not required.)

Place	Date	Hour	Summary of Events and Information	Remarks and references to Appendices
Hilgen.	1.8.19.		General Routine.	
	2.8.19.		The Band proceeded to Berg Gladbach to join the Massed Bands for the Divisional Tournament.	
	3.8.19.	1130.	Church Parade in Neuenhaus Church.	
	4.8.19.		General Holiday. The Commanding Officer, Lieut.Colonel W. J. J. Collas D.S.O., proceeded on leave.	
	5.8.19		-Athletic- The Battalion Annual/Sports, held at Dunweg – find day – Brigadier General H. Tindall Lucas, C.M.G., D.S.O. attended. A very successful day. Analysis of Sports:- "A" Company – 66 points. "B" Company – 50 points. "C" Company – 15 points. "D" Company – 20 points.	
	6.8.19		General Routine.	
	7.8.19.		General Routine.	
	8.8.19.		Divisional Tournament at Kalk. Special train for conveyance of troops from Hilgen to Kalk. Massed Bands consisting of all the Bands in Division.	
	9.8.19.		Divisional Tournament continued.	
	10.8.19.	1130.	Church Parade at Neuenhaus Church.	

Army Form C. 2118.

WAR DIARY
or
INTELLIGENCE SUMMARY.
(Erase heading not required.)

Instructions regarding War Diaries and Intelligence Summaries are contained in F. S. Regs., Part II. and the Staff Manual respectively. Title pages will be prepared in manuscript.

Place	Date	Hour	Summary of Events and Information	Remarks and references to Appendices
Hilgen.	11.8.19.		General Routine.	
	12.8.19.		General Routine.	
	13.8.19.		General Routine.	
	14.8.19.		Brigade Commander visited the Battalion.	
	15.8.19.		Advance Party to Dellbruck.	
Dellbruck.	16.8.19.		Battalion moved to Dellbruck for Musketry. Departed from Hilgen at 0830 marching via Dunweg, Schlebusch and Dunnwald. All in Camp by 1430 - Warm day. Dinners served on line of march.	
	17.8.19.		Preparing for Battalion to commence firing on Range.	
	18.8.19.		Battalion commenced firing Rhine Army Musketry Course, Part 1. "B" and "C" and Battalion Headquarter Company on Dellbruck Range.	
	19.8.19.		"A", "D" and Battalion Headquarter Companies on Range.	
	20.8.19.		"B", "C" and Battalion Headquarter Companies on Range.	
	21.8.19.		General Officer Commanding, 2nd Southern Infantry Brigade visited Battalion and inspected the Camp and saw the firing.	
	22.8.19.		Part II Musketry Course commenced by Battalion.	
	23.8.19.		Battalion on Range.	

Army Form C. 2118.

WAR DIARY
or
INTELLIGENCE SUMMARY.
(Erase heading not required.)

Instructions regarding War Diaries and Intelligence Summaries are contained in F.S. Regs., Part II. and the Staff Manual respectively. Title pages will be prepared in manuscript.

Place	Date	Hour	Summary of Events and Information	Remarks and references to Appendices
Dellbruck.	24.8.19.		Major G. T. Simcox D.S.O. to Brigade Headquarters. Conference on proposed Brigade Gymkhana to be held at Burscheid on 17th September.	
	25.8.19.		Parts 1 and 11 Musketry Course completed by Battalion.	
	26.8.19.		Part 111 Musketry Course commenced - Classification. Colonel H. Harslake G.S.O. 1. visited the Battalion on the Range. Southern Divisional Concert Party, "Fragments", visited the Battalion.	
	27.8.19.		Commanding Officer returned from Leave.	
	28.8.19.		Part 111 Musketry Course completed. Brigade Commander visited the Battalion.	
	29.8.19.		General Fatigues and Interior Economy.	
	30.8.19.		Battalion returned to Hilgen. Departed from Dellbruck at 0730. Arriving at 1200.	
Hilgen.	31.8.19.	1130.	Brigade Commander inspected Battalion on line of march. Church Parade at Neuenhaus Church.	

Army Form C. 2118.

WAR DIARY
or
INTELLIGENCE SUMMARY.
(Erase heading not required)

Instructions regarding War Diaries and Intelligence Summaries are contained in F.S. Regs., Part II. and the Staff Manual respectively. Title pages will be prepared in manuscript.

Place	Date	Hour	Summary of Events and Information	Remarks and references to Appendices
HINGEN.	1.9.19.		General Routine.	
	3.9.19.		General Routine.	
	3.9.19.		General Routine.	
	4.9.19.		Miss Ada Moore, British Empire Leave Club, and The "Green Diamonds" Concert Party (9th Durham L.I.) visited the Battalion.	
	5.9.19.		General Routine. Divisional Boxing Contest at BURSCHEID. Battalion defeated the team of D.115th Battery, R.F.A., by 2 points.	
	6.9.19.		5th Battalion's Annual Sports at BURSCHEID.	
	7.9.19.	1130.	Church Parade at NEUENHAUS Church. Band and Drums attended. Teams departed for Rhine Army Rifle Meeting at DROVE.	
	9.9.19.		The "Frongs" Concert Party visited the Battalion.	
	10.9.19.		Corps Boxing Championship - Southern Division V Light Division. 51st Bn. Devon Regt's Team represented Southern Division and defeated the Team of the 13th Bn. K.R.R., who represented the Light Division, by 2 points, thus qualifying for the Rhine Army Finals.	
	11.9.19.		General Routine.	
	13.9.19.		General Routine.	
	13.9.19.	1130.	Church Parade at NEUENHAUS Church. Band and Drums attended.	

Army Form C. 2118.

Sheet 2.

WAR DIARY
or
INTELLIGENCE SUMMARY.

(Erase heading not required.)

Place	Date	Hour	Summary of Events and Information	Remarks and references to Appendices
HILGEN.	13.9.19.		The Battalion Teams returned from the Rhine Army Rifle Meeting. Results:- Battalion Team Events. - Won by the Battalion. Silver Cup Awarded. Sergts Team. - 3rd Prize won by "B" Company. Lewis Gun Event. - 3rd Prize won by "B" Company. Fire Direction & Control.- 3rd Prize won by "A" Company. Individual Events. Prizes won by:- Captain C.L.G.Mackay-Forbes - 3rd. C.S.M. Broomfield. - 7th. 78548. Pte. Tall W.H."D"Coy.- 9th.	
	14.9.19.	1130	Church Parade at NEUENHAUS Church. Band and Drums attended.	
	15.9.19.		General Routine.	
	16.9.19.		The Commanding Officer, Lieut.Colonel H.J.J.Collas D.S.O., at Brigade Headquarters, to meet Commander-in-Chief, Rhine Army.	
	17.9.19.		Brigade Gymkhana at BURSCHEID. Battalion Band attended. Battalion Boxing Team fight in the Semi-finals of the Rhine Army Boxing Championships, winning 4 out of 7 fights.	
	18.9.19.		The Commanding Officer at Brigade Headquarters to meet the Corps Commander, Lieut.General Sir A.G.Godley, K.C.B., K.C.M.G.	

Army Form C. 2118.

Sheet 5.

WAR DIARY
or
INTELLIGENCE SUMMARY.

(Erase heading not required.)

Instructions regarding War Diaries and Intelligence Summaries are contained in F. S. Regs., Part II and the Staff Manual respectively. Title pages will be prepared in manuscript.

Place	Date	Hour	Summary of Events and Information	Remarks and references to Appendices
Hilgen.	18.9.19.		Rhine Army Boxing Championship Finals. The Battalion gained 3rd place with 18 points, the winners having 21 points and the second place was gained with 20 points.	
			Battalion individual winners:- Lieut. W. E. Hayes. Cpl. Pollard. C.	
			The Battalion Team fought right through the Competition with one short, thus being greatly handicapped. The following was the Team:-	
			Heavy Weight = Cpl. Pollard. Middle Weight = Pte. Sprayson. Welter " = Pte. Ham. Welter(Officers) = Lieut. W. E. Hayes. Light Weight = Sgt. Barker. Feather " = L/C. Sherry. Bantam " = Pte. Anthony.	
	19.9.19.		General Routine.	
	20.9.19.		General Routine.	
	21.9.19.	1120.	Church Parade at NEUENHAUS Church.	
	22.9.19.		Cricket Match between Southern Division and Light Division, Won by Southern Division. Scores:- Southern Division, 190. - Light Division, 180.	
	22.9.19.		General Routine.	
	23.9.19.		General Routine.	
	24.9.19.		General Routine.	

Army Form C. 2118.

Sheet 4.

WAR DIARY
or
INTELLIGENCE SUMMARY.
(Erase heading not required.)

Instructions regarding War Diaries and Intelligence Summaries are contained in F.S. Regs., Part II. and the Staff Manual respectively. Title pages will be prepared in manuscript.

Place	Date	Hour	Summary of Events and Information	Remarks and references to Appendices
	25.9.19.		Brigade Rhine Trip. Fine day, Battalion Band attended. Brigade Commander and his wife present.	
	26.9.19.		Preparing for move to BURG.	
	27.9.19.		The Battalion, less "C" Company, moves to BURG in relief of 52nd Battalion. Disposition:- "A" Company to Right Sector. "B" Company to Left Sector. "D" Company at BURG. H.Q.Company in the Schloss, BURG. The relief was completed by 1400. "C" Company proceeded to Prisoners of War Camp, DELLBRUCK, in relief of a Company of the 9th Bn. Gloucesters, to take over Guard Duties. The Company entrained at TENITE at 0500 and completed the relief by 1000.	
BURG.	28.9.19.		Church Parade in the Chapel in the Schloss at 0930.	
	29.9.19.		General Routine.	
	30.9.19.		A Board, of which Brigadier General B. R. Kirwan, C,B;, C.M.G., R.A., was President, accompanied by the Brigade Commander, inspected the Transport in connection with the Divisional Competition.	

Army Form C. 2118.

WAR DIARY
or
INTELLIGENCE SUMMARY.
(Erase heading not required.)

Instructions regarding War Diaries and Intelligence Summaries are contained in F. S. Regs., Part II. and the Staff Manual respectively. Title pages will be prepared in manuscript.

No. D.L.972.
51 Devons.

Place	Date	Hour	Summary of Events and Information	Remarks and references to Appendices
BURG.	1/10/19.		General Routine.	
BURG.	2/10/19.		General Routine.	
BURG.	3/10/19.		Commanding Officer to Brigade Headquarters.	
BURG.	4/10/19.		General Routine.	
BURG.	5/10/19.		Church Parade in Schloss Chapel, BURG. at 0930.	
BURG.	6/10/19.		General Routine.	
BURG.	7/10/19.		General routine.	
BURG.	8/10/19.		General Routine.	
BURG.	9/10/19.		General Routine. Orders received from Brigade that Battalion is to be disbanded. Brigade Commander, Brigadier General G.H.Tindall Lucas. C.M.G.,D.S.O. and Staff to dinner.	
BURG.	10/10/19.		General Routine.	
BURG.	11/10/19.		General Routine.	
BURG.	12/10/19.		Church Parade in Schloss Chapel, BURG at 0930. Brigade Commander departs for England.	
BURG.	13/10/19		General Routine.	
BURG.	14/10/19.		General Routine.	
BURG.	15/10/19.		General Routine.	

Army Form C. 2118.

WAR DIARY
or
INTELLIGENCE SUMMARY.
(Erase heading not required.)

Instructions regarding War Diaries and Intelligence Summaries are contained in F. S. Regs., Part II. and the Staff Manual respectively. Title pages will be prepared in manuscript.

Place	Date	Hour	Summary of Events and Information	Remarks and references to Appendices
BURG.	16/10/19		General Routine.	
BURG.	17/10/19.		General Routine.	
BURG.	18/10/19.		General Routine.	
BURG.	19/10/19.		Church Parade in Schloss Chapel, BURG., at 0930. Brigade Commander Lieut.Colonel.A.B.Ingledon Webber. C.M.G., D.S.O. visits Battalion. Orders received that unit will proceed from Rhine Army intact.	
BURG.	20/10/19.		Battalion prepares for move to BURSCHEID.	
BURG.	21/10/19.		Battalion moves to BURSCHEID via WERMELSKIRCHEN and HILGEN. All in at 1630. "C" Company rejoins Battalion from Prisoners of War Camp DELLBRUCK at 1500. Draft of 150 Other Ranks from 1/5th Bn. The Devonshire Regiment.	
BURSCHEID.	22/10/19.		General Interior Economy.	
BURSCHEID.	23/10/19.		General Routine.	
BURSCHEID.	24/11/19.		General Routine.	
BURSCHEID.	25/10/19.		General Routine.	
BURSCHEID.	26/10/19.		Church Parade in BURSCHEID Church at 1130.	
BURSCHEID.	27/10/19.		"B" Company proceeds to Prisoners of War Camp, DELLBRUCK in relief of a company of the 1/5th Bn. The Devonshire Regiment.	
BURSCHEID.	28/10/19.		Orders received for Battalion to take over Perimeter Line from BERGISCH BORN inclusive to KAISER WILHELM BRIDGE exclusive.	

Army Form C. 2118.

WAR DIARY
or
INTELLIGENCE SUMMARY.
(Erase heading not required.)

Instructions regarding War Diaries and Intelligence Summaries are contained in F. S. Regs., Part II. and the Staff Manual respectively. Title pages will be prepared in manuscript.

Place	Date	Hour	Summary of Events and Information	Remarks and references to Appendices
BURSCHEID.	28/10/19.		(continued).	
			Brigadier General D.E.Cayley, C.B., C.M.G. takes over command of 2nd Southern Infantry Brigade.	
BURSCHEID.	29/10/19.		Battalion moves to WERMELSKIRCHEN taking over the Perimeter from the 52nd Battalion The Devonshire Regiment and 1 Company of the 51st Battalion The Hampshire Regiment. Disposition of Battalion.-	
			Headquarters. "A" and "B" Company's. - WERMELSKIRCHEN.	
			" "C" Company. (right) = PREYERS MUHLE.	
			" "D" Company. (left) = WESTHAUSEN.	
WERMELSKIRCHEN.	30/10/19.		"B" Company rejoins Battalion from Prisoners of War Camp. DELLBRUCK.	
WERMELSKIRCHEN.	31/10/19.		Commanding Officer visits area of "C" Company.	
				[signature] ADJUTANT. 51st BATTN. DEVONSHIRE REGT.
			Commanding 51st Battalion The Devonshire Regiment... Lieutenant Colonel.